ARE WE THERE YET?
ALL ABOUT THE PLANET SATURN!
SPACE FOR KIDS
Children's Aeronautics & Space Book

BABY PROFESSOR

EDUCATION KIDS

Saturn is the sixth planet
in the Solar system.

Saturn is the
2nd biggest
planet in
our solar
system.

Saturn is also the lightest planet in our Solar System.

If there is a tub big enough to hold Saturn, it will just float in the water.

The distance
of Saturn
from the
Sun is
approximately
856 million
miles.

Saturn is
surrounded
by a system
of rings.
The rings
are 169,800
miles wide.

The rings
are made up
of particles
of ice, dust
and rocks.

The rings were discovered by Galileo Galilei in 1610 through a telescope.

Saturn is composed of hydrogen and helium.

Saturn is the
only planet
in our Solar
System that
is lighter
than water.

The diameter
of Saturn is
approximately
120,000
kilometers.

It takes
Saturn 29
and 1/2
years to
complete 1
revolution
around
the Sun.

Saturn has 62 confirmed moons. 53 of them have names.

Titan is the largest moon of Saturn and the second largest moon in our solar system.

The distance
to Saturn
from Earth
is around
746 million
miles.

Saturn's temperature is believed to be around -270 degrees Fahrenheit.

Saturn completes a full rotation in just about 10 hours.

Saturn's rings orbit at different speeds and have gaps between them.

Saturn is
the furthest
planet that
can be seen
with just the
naked eye.

Visit
BABY PROFESSOR
EDUCATION KIDS
www.BabyProfessorBooks.com
to download Free Baby Professor eBooks
and view our catalog of new and exciting
Children's Books